Elvira Haskins Holloway

Gleanings from the Golden State

Elvira Haskins Holloway

Gleanings from the Golden State

ISBN/EAN: 9783743311954

Manufactured in Europe, USA, Canada, Australia, Japa

Cover: Foto ©ninafisch / pixelio.de

Manufactured and distributed by brebook publishing software
(www.brebook.com)

Elvira Haskins Holloway

Gleanings from the Golden State

Preface.

IN the pages of this book, as the title indicates, are glimpses of the beautiful State of California ; glimpses of her sublime and picturesque scenery ; of her majestic mountains, her noble forests, her mighty cataracts, and natural wonders of the Yosemite Valley ; her beautiful lakes that gem the mountains, her mines of virgin gold, her grand and beautiful rivers, her magnificent harbors, her wide-stretching fertile valleys, her fruitful vineyards and her orange groves ; her vast domain of everything lovely in Nature, where all the tints of the most beautiful skies that have ever been are seen ; the emeralds of all the seas, glorified with the silver light of celestial stars ; the glowing purples of all the hills, the exquisite radiance of Orient dawns, the magnificent splendors of golden sunsets, and the ten thousand rainbow glories of the beautiful flowers, strewn with a prodigal hand over this broad Empire of the " Golden West ! "

ELVIRA H. HOLLOWAY.

Thanks.

To the OVERLAND MONTHLY, the OAKLAND HOME INSURANCE Co., and others who generously assisted the writer with illustrations for this volume, I desire in this public manner to express my earnest thanks and grateful appreciation.

Also sincere and grateful thanks to Miss BAKER for the figurative, artistic design of the frontispiece.

Very sincerely,

E. H. H.

"QUEEN OF THE PACIFIC."

"Queen of the Pacific."

A Queen beside the Western Sea
Awaits a glorious destiny:

Her sandals flecked with glistening spray,
From white-caps tossing on the bay.

Her face uplifted, like a star,
Gleaming above the heights afar;

She guards the commerce of the sea,
And waits her glories yet to be!

Upon her brow a crown of gold
That sunset rays with glory rolled;

Her purple garments trailing o'er
The silver sands along the shore;

Her vesture broidered o'er with flowers
From nature's lovely fragrant bowers,

She thus in proud array doth wait,
Enthroned within the Golden Gate.

From coffers rich at her command,
Bestows her wealth with gracious hand;

Where e'er distress is hovering nigh,
Her golden eagles quickly fly!

While nations far and near, I ween,
Pay tribute to Pacific's Queen.

California.

Amid the beauty of the sunsets beside the Western sea,
There is a land of glorious promise,—fair California!
Where, with majestic grandeur mountains lift their summits high,
Unto the azure realms of a peerless, sunlit sky:
And purple walled they stand amid the sunset's golden glow,
Looking down on grand old forests and the ocean far below.

Looking down on wave-like hills, sleeping amid the dreamy calm
Of the beauteous summer time, and on the stately palm,
With green fronds rustling in the breeze wafted from o'er the sea,
With balmy breath of odors sweet, from far off India;—
While Flora smiles with wealth of bloom, with grace and beauty rare,
Crowning the hills and sunny vales with garlands fresh and fair.

Her silken tresses rivaling the sunbeam's molten glow,
Wreathed o'er with amaranths that bloom near mountains veiled
                    with snow;
With lilies of the valley twined with roses fair and sweet,
And purple heather blooms from Diablo's vine-clad feet;
Her trailing emerald robe with meadow daisies starred;—
She walks in sunshine o'er the hills, her banner crimson barred.

Looking down on fertile valleys, over fields of waving grain,
On golden-fruited orange groves that skirt her vast domain,
On orchards with their scented bloom, and on the thrifty vines
That bear rich promise of the yield of sparkling ruby wines,
On crystal streams that flow o'er gleaming golden sand,
On singing rills and fountains that rejoice the grateful land,

SANTA BARBARA, SOUTHERN CALIFORNIA.

LICK OBSERVATORY ON MOUNT HAMILTON.

" Proud Science on Mount Hamilton has made her lofty home,
   Searching for unknown worlds of light through heaven's jeweled dome."

Where Pomona walks with pride at the harvest's golden prime,
Bestowing gracious gifts from this semi-tropic clime :
With purple clusters of the vine, and orange blossoms fair,
With olives green, entwined in her burnished nut-brown hair ;
Her silken banner waving through fields of tasseled corn,
Festooned with garlands flamed with the orient beams of morn.

Among the rocky battlements are gold and silver mines,
Where the pioneer has wrought and dreamed beneath the swaying
        pines.
Broad rivers from the cañons flowing down to meet the sea,
Bear ships and barges laden with the fruits of industry.
Within these haunts Pan trills his pipe amid the insects' hum.
Where the pheasant wakes all living things, at daybreak with her
        drum.

The " Sierras " guard in serried ranks the eastern gates of day,
While Mount Diablo guards the west, three hundred miles away !
Proud Science on Mount Hamilton has made her lofty home,
Searching for unknown worlds of light, through heaven's jeweled
        dome.
Mount Tamalpais watchful stands beside the Golden Gate,
And grand old Shasta, throned and crowned, guards all the vast
        estate !

MOUNT SHASTA.

" Grand old Shasta, throned and crowned,
  Guards all the vast estate ' "

Mount Shasta After a Storm.

The storm has passed, and swift clouds roll by
With graceful pennons through the wind-swept sky,
Drifting fair and clear in billowy white,
As the sun shines forth with mellow light.

Like a gallant ship that outrides the storm,
Shasta towers serene with majestic form,
Her massive, snow-crowned, rock-heaved, shining crest
Rising high above the ocean's billowy breast.

Thus grandly sculptured on a colossal throne,
Her summit tow'rs above the forest's verdant zone,
With majesty sublime to the bending skies, —
While far below the vale of summer lies.

Admission of California

TO THE UNION, SEPTEMBER 9, 1850.

Rejoice ye sisters of the Stately band,
  Who meet in council at Columbia's knee,
There cometh one, with wealth of golden land
  Washed by the billows of the sunset sea.

In gala dress she comes, with hair of gold
  That veils her with its shining tresses o'er.
Down to her jeweled feet of peerless mold,
  With sandals wrought as Incas were of yore.

She comes with gracious manners free from guile,
  Like Sheba's queen, across her fertile plains!
With loyal heart and beaming, genial smile,
  Proffers rich gifts of ripened fruits and grains.

With jeweled fingers proffers her red wine
  That all may drink to labor and success,
Drink to the brotherhood of all mankind!
  To love that wins them, and to deeds that bless.

Golden Poppies.

(THE ESCHSCHOLTZIA.)

Gay, satin blooms of lustrous sheen
Garland the hills and meadows green;
And dainty bits of color fling,
As in the breeze they nod and swing,
Above the greensward to and fro,
While fleeting shadows come and go.

Wild birds and bees and butterflies
Sing o'er them low, sweet lullabies,
Sipping the raindrops and the dew
From out their cups of golden hue
Lifted upon the mountain side,
And o'er the green fields stretching wide.

The floral emblem of the State
That borders on the Golden Gate:
Unfolding in the gleaming rays
Of sunshine, crowning all the days
Of summer's mellow atmosphere,
A bright-hued, golden pioneer.

"THREE GRACES," YOSEMITE.

Yosemite Valley.

A beautiful valley, a wonderful land,
That Nature has fashioned with masterful hand!
With sheer massive cliffs forming high granite walls,
With towering domes and magnificent falls!
With booming cascades that in swift torrents leap
Over high battlements, down the rocky steep,
Dashing and swirling, tossing glistening spray
Of feathery foam. Lovely fountains at play,
Like the plumes of white clouds becalmed in the sky,
When zephyrs float softly on noiseless wings by.

There are beautiful rocks with turrets and spires,
That are bronzed with the sunset's smoldering fires!
And the river Merced with calm beauty flows
Through green groves and meadows, where shadows repose
In the waters that mirror along the shore,
With picturesque beauty green boughs arching o'er.
There the robin's clear notes of sweet minstrelsy
Are oft heard from each sylvan bower and tree,
From the odorous pines on the woodland hills,
And in fair, shady nooks by the laughing rills.

Joined in mystic union the Three Brothers stand,
In a vast mountain building that Nature planned;
And the faithful Guardsmen, with majestic form,
Keep their silent watches through sunshine and storm,—
Through the long summer's heat and the winter's snow,
As the changing seasons ever come and go.
And the circling years pass with a tireless pace;
The lengthening shadows at eventide trace;
The diurnal passing of Time in his flight,
With the radiant sunsets, on wings of light

The Great Architect with munificence planned
This beautiful temple, majestic and grand!
And glorious anthems that quicken the soul,
Through broad, winding aisles with sublime music roll
To the high arching dome among lofty towers,
And through leafy cloisters fragrant with flowers,—
Where the beauteous wealth of the passion vine
Around glowing altars their sweet blossoms twine,—
While the faint heard chime of the distant cascade
Tinkles gently afar through the sylvan glade.

MIRROR LAKE.

Mirror Lake.

Nature's beautiful mirror! When evening draws near,
In thy waters her radiant glories appear;
On thy calm, peerless bosom fair Luna reclines,
And the bright, starry bridge of the "milky way" shines
With silvery rays from the archway of heaven,
And a glimpse of two worlds is in duplicate given.

The calm "Breath Divine" o'er thy still waters flowing,
Is borne on the zephyrs the soft winds are blowing;
And the crystal wavelets of thy glistening rings
Are the moving circles made by viewless wings,
When the spirits of Silence and Peace hover there,
In the hush of the noontime of night in the air.

As the silvery stars at the dawn's early gleam,
From a clear, stainless sky o'er thy blest waters beam,
The rock-ribbed summits of lofty mountains are seen
Inverted below with the green woods between,
Where soft zephyrs woo plumy boughs arching o'er
With picturesque beauty, thy bordering shore.

As the morning light dawns, a magnificent scene
Is exquisitely penciled in thy crystal sheen!
And the great golden ball flushing orient heights,
Shoots his ambushed arrows gilt with burnished lights,
On the high fronting cliffs, while glowing tints and shades
Are reflected through gorges and deep everglades.

A beautiful halo, ineffably bright,
Transfigures thy heav'n-painted canvas with light!
And the verdure-framed picture beheld with rapt gaze,
Is aflame with the splendor of dawn's glowing rays—
An exquisite painting that Nature has wrought,
Resplendent with beauty the sunlight has caught.

Mount Tamalpais.

With lofty grandeur Tamalpais
Is looking down from high estate,
Over the broad Pacific's strand
And harbor of the Golden Gate.

Upon a firm-built, rocky throne,
With triple crowns this monarch stands
A sturdy bulwark by the sea,
Guarding the realm of fertile lands.

Holding the ocean winds at bay
That lash with fury all the main!
Lifting its beetling front to heaven
That storms may never reach the plain.

There, looking down from cloud-wreathed skies
When winds are blowing wild and free,
Fair vales in tranquil beauty lie
Nestled within the sheltering lee.

When waves roll high, with surging boom
Bold breakers climb its rugged breast,
And round its base the tides make moan
While balmy vales 'neath sunshine rest.

No monarch guards a lovelier realm
'Neath brighter skies beyond the sea,
Nor zephyrs whisper sweeter tones
To flowers that gem the verdant lea.

From winding paths on heights sublime
The broad horizon meets the view,
A panorama vast and grand
Beneath God's canopy of blue.

There through immensity of space
A vision greets the wondering gaze,
That thrills the soul with reverent awe,
And moves the heart with fervent praise.

Three centuries of time have passed
Since the explorers landed here—
Cabrillo, and Sir Francis Drake
The first to find the harbors near.

The first white men who trod the sands
Of California's wave-washed shore!
Who dreamed not of her wealth of lands,
Or treasures vast of golden ore.

And looking backward o'er the years,
To me, the wondrous changes seem
As strange as those by fancies wrought,
In Bellamy's romantic dream.

For lo, the commerce of the world
Finds entrance through the Golden Gate!
And Freedom's star-eyed priestess guards
The helm that guides the "Ship of State."

Far in the west the sunset skies
Gleam o'er the ocean's wide expanse,
And crimson waves of sea and sky
Do meet and mingle with the glance.

In Nature's drama, Tamalpais
Acts well a generous, noble part,
Teaching that *greatness* is endowed
With gracious kindliness of heart.

Point Reyes Harbor.

Three hundred circling years have passed
    Since first a Saxon crossed the sea,
And anchored safely at Point Reyes,
    Within the harbor's sheltered lea.

A hero from Great Britain's Isle,—
    A valiant man of noble birth,
Who in the good ship Golden Hind
    " Did plow a furrow round the earth."

Sir Francis Drake, who trod the sands
    Of California's wave-washed shore ;
Who knew not of the fertile lands,
    Or bounteous wealth of golden ore.

Who sailed away and knew not of
    The harbor of the Golden Gate;
Nor dreamed he of the future fame,
    Or wealth, or grandeur of the State.

"Lone Cypress Tree."

(NEAR MONTEREY.)

On a rock in the ocean the lone cypress stands,
Like the mountain that rises amid arid sands;
Like the fountain that flows with clear, singing rill,
From the bare rock that gleams on the crest of the hill;
Like the stream that burst forth in the desolate wild,
Where sad Hagar roamed with her innocent child.

Like the love that survives neglect's blighting power,
Like the friendship that lives through misfortune's dark hour;
Like the hopes that are born of the waves of despair,
That green cypress tree is a harbinger fair!
Like an anchor it rests on the rock in the sea,
While the winds breathe around it their wild symphony.

VIEW OF MARKET STREET, SAN FRANCISCO, SHOWING TWIN PEAKS
IN THE DISTANCE.

" And glowing clouds the ' Twin Peaks ' kiss
When falls the curtain of the night."

The "Twin Peaks" of Mt. Dolores.

(SAN FRANCISCO.)

The mountain, with its verdant peaks,
  Stands sentry near the ocean shore :
Guarding the vale where roses creep
  With clustering vines the lattice o'er.

The feathery palm with beauty grows
  Among the roses sweet and fair,
And lovely calla lilies bloom,
  With fragrance in the balmy air.

By fresh'ning breeze from o'er the sea
  The plumy palms are gently fanned.
When white-capped waves, with wanton glee,
  Toss foam-wreathed spray along the strand.

At sunset's hour, bright golden rays
  Illumine vale and mountain height :
And glowing clouds the " Twin Peaks " kiss,
  When falls the curtain of the night.

The watching stars are peeping through
  With twinkling smiles, that seem to say,
" We saw the blushing clouds that passed
  Kiss verdant hills, then float away."

The Sunbeam's Wooing.

The sunbeam followed the moonbeam
  Through meadow, vale and glen,
Into the darkling forest,
  Far from the haunts of men.

The pale and trembling moonbeam
  Stole into the dense green shade,
And through dim aisles and cloisters
  With wavering glances strayed.

The sunbeam softly followed
  Into a vine-wreathed bower,
Where the moonbeam's quivering glances
  Fell in a silver shower.

The sunbeam caught the glances,
  And clasped in a warm embrace
The lovely trembling moonbeam,
  As she hid her shy, pale face.

Mission Dolores.

A quaint adobe structure, built
   With an arched door of ancient style;
Tiled roof, and windows small and high—
   A rude, but reminiscent pile.

High in the storied arches rang
   With vesper chimes, the " Mission bells ;"
And of the years, a century
   Of silver tones, the record tells!

A marble tablet bears the name
   Of one who near the ocean sleeps,
The founder of this ancient church,
   O'er which the green-leaved ivy creeps.

Now silence reigns within the walls,
   Where voices chanted music sweet :
But Mount Dolores guards alway
   This antique temple at her feet.

GOLDEN GATE PARK.

" There in profusion lovely flowers
With fragrance scent the ambient air "

Golden Gate Park.

Where sand dunes piled beside the sea,
  Drifted by winds and ebbing tide,
A lovely park now meets the view,
  That is the city's boast and pride.

There in profusion lovely flowers
  With fragrance scent the ambient air,
And rare exotics breathe perfume
  In bowers wreathed with garlands fair.

O'er feathery ferns and plumy palms,
  Bright fountains in the sunshine play:
And mosses cling round tropic vines,
  Beneath the iris tinted spray.

And sculptured statues grace the scene,
  Wrought by the artist's skillful hand
In memory of our honored dead—
  Brave heroes of this chosen land.

One is the likeness of a bard,
  Francis Scott Key, the poet's name:
Our starry banner was the theme
  That won for him immortal fame.

Another bears the honored name
  Of one who was our country's pride:
From duty's path he never swerved—
  The Nation wept when Garfield died.

CLIFF HOUSE AND SEAL ROCKS.

" We stood on the heights in the gloaming,
  Gazing out o'er the restless sea."

Ocean Waves.

We stood on the heights in the gloaming,
  Gazing out o'er the restless sea;
" Oh, what are the wild waves saying?"
  A laughing voice whispered to me.

" My dear, if you listen attentive,
  You can hear what the ocean waves say,
As they break on the shore with low murmur,
  Or dance lightly in sportive play."

The fair, glowing face was a picture,
  As she watched, with eyes opened wide,
The white-capped waves that were dancing
  In the arms of the ocean tide.

" I can hear what the waves are saying,
  As they bound o'er the waters free ;
They bear from the mystic islands
  A sweet message of hope to me."

MOUNT DIABLO.

On the Heights.

The cool, salt air blew o'er their faces,
  As hand in hand they stood on the height :
Before them the throbbing waste of waters,
  And sunset sky of crimson light.

A white sail gleams in the far horizon,
  Where flaming sky and ocean meet :
Along the shore white waves are breaking
  Against the rocks beneath their feet.

The crimson waves of sunset glory
  Are fading over sea and land ;
The last bright rays the waves are kissing,
  The waves return and kiss the strand.

Is it a dream that I remember,
  Those two, alone, in the waning light?
The ocean waves and sunset splendor,
  Or gleaming sails of the ship in sight?

Point.

"CROSSING THE BAY,"

Crossing the Bay of San Francisco.

(NOVEMBER 11, 1896.)

Small boats are gliding o'er the bay,
   And ships are sailing out to sea ;
One with broad sails, like drifted snow,
   Is bound for far-off India.

The wavelets dance with rippling glee
   To meet the sun's bright glancing ray,
And sea gulls whirl and circling skim
   The gleaming surface of the bay.

The coast range in the distance lies,
   With outline of celestial blue ;
And Fort Point, with its arsenal
   Of mounted guns. recedes from view.

And out beyond the Oakland pier,
   The vernal hills among,
Are tall church spires that heavenward point,
   Where golden clouds are hung.

OAKLAND HOME INSURANCE CO. BUILDING.

VIEW OF OAKLAND.

Oakland.

From Oakland's vernal, wave-like hills,
  Comes the breath of summer flowers :
Where sunbeams with the shadows play,
  Through the fleeting, golden hours.

The dreamy hills are sloping down,
  To meet the green fields stretching wide.
Through glades of oak, round curving roads,
  Wind crystal streams with silver tide.

The coast range girdles field and plain
  Outlined along the far confines ;
Upon their rugged, craggy slopes,
  Soft breezes woo the dusky pines.

The sun drops down, a golden crown,
  Upon the waters of the bay :
Then slowly sinks in crimson skies,
  As twilight dons her mantle gray.

The cool, salt breeze from o'er the sea,
  Wafts echoes from the signal gun ;
Now swallows to their nestlings fly,
  And daily tasks of toil are done.

LAKE MERRITT.

" Nestled among the dreamy hills
The quiet waters slumb'rous lie."

Lake Merritt.

Nestled among the dreamy hills
  The quiet waters slumb'rous lie,
With sunbeams flashing o'er the brim,
  From out the sapphire-tinted sky.

The vernal hills, from grassy slopes,
  Reach down to where the wavelets leap
To meet the light winds as they pass,
  And through the rustling hedge rows creep.

White sail boats, with broad canvas spread,
  Over the gleaming surface skim
Like white plumed birds, with graceful sweep.
  Circling around the silver rim.

The wanton breeze ripples the leaves
  Of stately oaks, that skirt the shore ;
And wild birds to their nestlings sing,
  High in the branches leaning o'er.

SUNSET AT LAKE TAHOE.

" And burnished rays with splendor crown
Lake Tahoe as the sun goes down.

Sunset at Lake Tahoe.

With twinkling light the vesper star
Shone in the horizon, afar ;
And glowing rays of mellow light
Were streaming o'er the mountain height.

And, as fair evening nearer came,
She threw her amber robe of flame
O'er all she passed, till shore and height
Were radiant with the crimson light.

Across the west, with gleaming hand
She stretched a flaming purple band ;
And all the glittering sand stained o'er
With rainbow hues along the shore.

The bordering hills and mountains glow
With brilliant hues, that flash below ;
Their shaggy slopes, from tow'ring height,
Transfigured with the golden light.

The burnished arrows, darting through
The lofty pines of emerald hue,
Illumine dusky aisles that glow,
Mirrored within the lake below.

Now golden arrows flash and gleam,
And o'er the crystal waters seem
To shine with a resplendent crown
Of brightness, as the sun goes down.

Ere shadows make the twilight dim,
Close to the water's azure rim
There leaps a line of smoldering fire,
That gleams like a cathedral spire.

Methinks I hear the vesper's chime,
And see the altar's votive shrine ;
Then twilight kneels devoutly there,
And night ascends day's golden stair.

She flings her mantle, gemmed with stars,
Across the sunset's crimson bars ;
And burnished rays with splendor crown
Lake Tahoe as the sun goes down.

Fallen Leaf Lake.

A lovely emerald lake, that nature's fairest mood
With sylvan beauty framed, by mountain, rock and wood ;
Where happy song birds chant their joyous, tuneful lay,
And softly calls the wood dove in the twilight gray,
When gentle zephyrs fan the mountain's rugged brow,
And whisper through the pine tree's verdant, rhythmic bough.

Lotta's Fountain.

(MARKET ST., SAN FRANCISCO.)

The ancient story runs that once a man
  Who found a spring within a desert bare,
  Scooped out a well, and walled it in with care.
And then, in furtherance of his kindly plan,
  A ladle wrought, and hung it on the brink,
  That from this well the thirsty traveler might drink.

Thus, in our time, a woman's thoughtful brain
  Conceived a kindly, generous deed, to bless
  The passer-by, who with the throng might press
Along the dusty street, intent to drain
  The cup at Lotta's fountain, flowing free
  To all who thirst within its boundary.

And oft beneath the noontide's glaring ray
  The passing stranger pauses there, to scan
  The handiwork of this most gracious plan
To cheer the toiler on his weary way ;
  Meanwhile ascends a grateful blessing there
  For Lotta's generous gift on the city's thoroughfare.

The Native Sons and Daughters

OF THE GOLDEN WEST.

In days of yore, the Indian roamed
With savage instinct, fierce and wild,
Through dense, vast, sunless forests, where,
Amid the tangled, steep defile
Of mountain pass, the grizzly bear
Was hunted in his secret lair.

Now, from the mountains to the sea,
The sturdy pioneer has made
A garden of this wilderness;
Admitting to the gloomy shade
And fertile soil the sun's caress,
Robing the earth with loveliness.

The mellow sun and balmy air
Ripens the fruits o'er hill and plain;
Flaming with ruddy glow the vines,
Tinging with gold the waving grain;
While in the depth of secret mines
With wealth of ore, the nugget shines.

With lightning chained to progress' car,
Across the prairies heralds fly;
The iron horse plows through the dome
Of tunneled mountains, grand and high;
And with swift speed the coursers roam,
While reapers gather harvests home.

With grateful pride and fealty,
The native sons and daughters wear,
As an emblem of the "Golden West,"
A nugget, which the grizzly bear
Hugs close to his broad, shaggy breast
As California's proud crest!

A FORTY-NINER PROSPECTING.

The Pioneers of California.

From o'er the seas, brave argonauts and bold
  Sailed through the burnished highway of the State,
In search of treasures deep in mines of gold,
  With varied plans, and hearts with hope elate.

And others "crossed the plains," o'er arid sands,
  To reach the Eldorado of the West!
Encountered savage foes in hostile bands,
  And braved the mountain pass and rocky crest.

In deep ravines, and leaping, singing rills,
  The river's bed, and on the winding shore,
The miner wrought and tunneled through the hills,
  Then freely gave from out his golden store.

The farmer tilled the soil with frugal hand,
  Where late had roamed the bison and the deer;
And reaped as he had sown—a harvest grand
  His faithful toil rewarding, year by year.

Now Ceres guards, through autumn's mellow prime,
  The hills and valleys of this fruitful land;
From bounteous stores of corn, and oil, and wine,
  Pours out full measure with unstinted hand.

And from the mountains to the sundown sea,
  Minerva's temples rise with lofty dome;
Her halls of science, art and learning free,
  To all who seek in this fair land a home.

A heritage of grand and noble deeds
  Wrought by the bold, intrepid pioneer,
Who wisely planned and built for future needs—
  The argonauts whose memory we revere.

DESCRIPTIVE NOTES.

Yosemite.—The Yosemite Valley is a cleft or gorge in the granite peak of the Sierra Nevada, situated in Mariposa County, California, 150 miles nearly due east from San Francisco.

The name Yosemite signifies "full-grown grizzly bear." The floor of the Valley, from Mirror Lake to El Capitan, ranging from half a mile to a mile in width, is level and charmingly wooded, with stretches of meadow lands, and knolls of oak and maple. Through the center of this park, with many an eddying curve, runs the Merced River, a clean, pebble-banked stream, where cloud shadows from off the high domes love to linger.

The Valley is seven miles long and a mile in height. Cloud's Rest is 10,000 feet in height; the North Dome, 7,568 feet; El Capitan, 7,300 feet; Cathedral Rocks, 6,660 feet; Three Brothers, 7,830 feet; Yosemite Falls, 2,700 feet; Bridal Veil Fall, 900 feet; Vernal Fall, 475 feet.

Tamalpais.—Looking northward from Telegraph Hill across the bay of San Francisco, Mt. Tamalpais is seen standing with bold front outlined against the blue sky, a majestic bulwark by the sea, rising 2,700 feet distinct and clear above the water. Its profile, which forms the sleeping beauty Elaine, extends along the entire coast of Marin County. This mountain sheltered the explorers Cabrillo and Sir Francis Drake, the first white men to approach the Golden Gate. Drake was the first Saxon to visit the shores of California. June 17, 1579, he sought shelter at Point Reyes Harbor, where he tarried thirty-six days, repairing and refitting his ship the Golden Hind, in which he sailed round the earth. Cabrillo landed in the same harbor in the year 1542.

Lake Tahoe.—Tahoe is the grandest of all the Sierra Lakes, lying partly in California and partly in Nevada. It is twenty-five miles in length, and in some places is from twelve to fifteen miles in width. It has a depth of 1,700 feet, an altitude of 6,220 feet, and is surrounded by mountains, which tower above the lake from 2,000 to nearly 5,000 feet. The water is clear as crystal. There is grandeur and enchantment at all times in the scenery which environs the lake. The summer sunsets upon Tahoe are remarkable for their great beauty and wealth of coloring, that no artist can paint.

Mirror Lake is a beautiful sheet of water, clear as crystal, at the foot of North Dome in the Yosemite Valley. It is the most beautiful lake in the world, and the environments are picturesque and sublime.

Mission Dolores.—This Chapel was dedicated November 9, 1776, by Father Junipero Serra, amid the firing of guns. While the Chapel was being built, a bell was brought from Mexico that had been cast in Mendoza, Spain, of gold and silver, in the year 1192.

The morning of November 9, just a few months after the Independence bell rang out its glad tidings of liberty, this bell rang out in clear, resonant silver tones, rejoicing the hearts of the soldiers, who recalled the scenes of old Spain and Mexico.

In 1802, two silver bells that were molded in 1797 were suspended, one on the right, and the other on the left of the smaller bell already placed on the day of the dedication. The interior of the Chapel is simple but interesting. The altar is modern. The statues are of adobe, but the gilding and painting are modern.

Sierra Nevada Mountains.—According to the State Geological Survey, there is an area of about 200 square miles in this section that has an elevation of about 8,000 feet, with over 100 peaks that rise above 10,000 feet, a score reaching 12,500 feet, and several over 14,000 feet. On the western slope of the High Sierra region, nature seems to have clustered the greatest of her California scenic wonders—scenery both grand and varied, solitary and magnificent, including the Yosemite and the Sequoia. Scattered along from Tehachapi to Tahoe are ice carved cañons, glaciers, time-eroded crags, frost-riven pinnacles, spires of granite and cliffs of basalt, beds of lava, sounding waterfalls and silent lakes, grand pine palisades, and beetling cliffs. There are beautiful streams in almost every square mile of its area, culminating in the mighty rivers of the San Joaquin and the Sacramento.

Lake Tahoe is the bright particular gem of the Sierra.

Mount Shasta.—Shasta is the crowning glory of the north, and from all sides is overpowering in its grandeur. Half its slopes are of evergreen and half of snow, and is the grand, towering landmark of the Sierras in the north, and has no rival within a radius of fifty miles. It is 14,440 feet in height.

www.ingramcontent.com/pod-product-compliance
Lightning Source LLC
Chambersburg PA
CBHW032133080426
42733CB00008B/1052